BLACK & WHITE

Bira Fonseca

Copyright © 2021 Bira Fonseca (also known as Bishop Joshua)

Second Edition. ISBN: 978-0-578-88854-5
Published by The Universal Church, Inc.
100 Mulberry Street, 14th Floor, Newark, NJ 07105

All rights reserved. No part of this book may be reproduced or transmitted in any form or by any means, electronic or mechanical, including photocopying or recording, or any information storage and retrieval system without permission in writing from the author.

First edition published in December 2019 by Editorial Planeta Mexicana, S.A. de C.V. bajo el sello editorial PLANETA M.R.
First Edition's ISBN: 978-607-07-6496-7

All Scripture quotations in this book were taken from the New King James Bible Version. Copyright © 1982 by Thomas Nelson. Used by permission. All rights reserved.

Photo and illustrations credits:
Cover, hand: Christos Georghiou/Shutterstock.com. Modified from original.
Page IX, top: Alex Staroseltsev/Shutterstock.com. Desaturated from original.
Page IX, bottom: humbak/Shutterstock.com. Desaturated from original.
Page 1 and recurring: gst/Shutterstock.com. Desaturated from original.
Page 3: Jag_cz/Shutterstock.com. Desaturated and modified.
Page 27 and recurring: valeriya kozoriz/Shutterstock.com
Page 28, top: John Gomez/Shutterstock.com. Desaturated from original.
Page 28, bottom: Oleg Golovnev/Shutterstock.com.
Page 30: Majivecka/Shutterstock.com. Modified from original.
Page 30: Black creator 24/Shutterstock.com
Page 45: David Pisnoy on Unsplash. Desaturated and modified from original.
Page 77: irabel8/Shutterstock.com. Desaturated and modified from original.
Page 92: TTstudio/Shutterstock.com. Desaturated and modified.
Pages 116, 117, 147: Bira Fonseca Family Collection
Page 149 icons: Dikas Space/Shutterstock.com

Printed by Nx Media, Inc.
6118 Aletha Lane, Houston, TX 77081

Printed in the United States of America

To the Spirit of Faith, Who believes in me and guides me every step of the way, and to my dear wife Ima and our children.

Contents

Introduction 1

CHAPTER 1: The Soul Has No Color 5
   Prejudice from Others 6
   Discrimination 7
   Racism 8
   Children Are Not Born Racist 10
   My Experiences Growing Up 11
   Will Discrimination Always Exist? 14
   Reactions 15
   Exercise Your Rights 20
   Do Not Use the Strength of Your Arms 23
   Food for Thought 27

CHAPTER 2: Mental Slavery 29
   SOS Self-Discrimination 30
   Freedom and Victory 33
   How to Be Free Within 39
   Food for Thought 43

CHAPTER 3: The Greatest Tool to Overcome Discrimination and Racism — 47

What Is Intelligent Faith? — 48

Intelligent Faith Leads to Freedom — 54

How to Overcome Prejudice Through Intelligent Faith — 55

Your Fifty Percent — 62

Faith in God and Faith in Yourself — 67

The Holy Spirit – The Spirit of Faith — 71

Food for Thought — 76

CHAPTER 4: The Greatest Obstacle to Intelligent Faith — 79

Emotions and Music — 80

Emotions and Religion — 85

The Holy Spirit and Emotions — 88

Placing Emotions in the Right Place — 93

Food for Thought — 95

CHAPTER 5: Your Identity and Behavior — 97

Body Language and What it Says About You — 102

Other People's Perceptions — 105

Be Yourself – Authenticity, Sincerity — **107**

How to Invest in Yourself — **108**

Food for Thought — **113**

CHAPTER 6: Next Generation — **115**

My Family — **118**

Investing in Your Family Is Investing in Your Heritage — **120**

Food for Thought — **125**

CHAPTER 7: Writing a New Story — **127**

Leave the Past Behind and Look Ahead — **128**

Work on Your Present — **133**

Good Lemonade — **134**

Put God First — **135**

Put Your Goals in Writing — **137**

Make a Plan — **138**

Move Ahead and Do Not Draw Back — **139**

Food for Thought — **141**

It Is Just the Beginning — **143**

Introduction

Perhaps you have been offended based on the color of your skin, or you have offended other people because you feel superior to them. I want to speak to you regardless of the color of your skin, origin, or background. The soul has no color. So before accusing or passing judgment on others, I would like for you to do and understand one thing: look at the content and do not judge by appearances.

How often have you bought a piece of fruit that looked appealing on the outside, but after cutting it, you noticed that the inside was rotten? Likewise, perhaps you have preconceived ideas about people based on what you see on the outside. You might even get involved in a romantic relationship because of these ideas, but when you get to know the person better, you realize that they are rotten inside; their character "stinks." Do not judge by appearances. Look into the content of others and invest in your own content and character. In this book, you will learn the tools to not only overcome prejudice, but also to believe and invest in yourself as a person and as a soul. You CAN succeed and be happy!

THE Soul HAS NO COLOR

The Soul Has No Color

The truth is that our soul has no color. We are who we are regardless of the color of our skin. Your soul, the essence of who you are, is not bound to your origin, nationality, height, weight, abilities, or so-called physical deformities. It is not restricted to a medical condition or your family history. Your soul is not defined by the tone of your skin or any physical characteristic: it is who you are, regardless of what others think or say of you.

Loving and accepting who you are is a key step to your success. For you to move forward and persevere in your goals regardless of circumstances, you must believe in yourself. Over time our bodies age, and eventually all that former strength fades away. What you think, what you do, and the choices you make in life are what will continue and remain in your old age and for future generations. Your life is the result of what you think. Your thoughts are what lead you to take action. The question is: what do you think about yourself? Do you believe in and value yourself?

Let's analyze some of the things that you will eventually face in life and the ways you can stay true to who you are and invest in yourself. After all, we invest in what we believe.

Prejudice from Others

Prejudice is an irrational and unreasonable idea or feeling towards a person or a group of people which is not based on facts. It can cause positive feelings or rejection towards someone based on their appearance, background, origin, or any other distinction without the appropriate knowledge.

It is impossible to go through life and interact with people without facing prejudice at one time or another. A lack of knowledge and misinformation are the two main factors behind prejudice. When people do not know the facts, they usually do one of three things: they believe what others say, they make assumptions, or they look for the facts. The truth is that very few people today search for valid information.

The best way to deal with prejudice is to inform people of the truth. The best way to do this is by allowing people to get to know you better and understand your story; by being truthful and honest to who you are and not allowing others' prejudices to shape your thoughts and behavior. In this book you will learn how to accomplish this... because you can!

Discrimination

Here we will refer to "discrimination" as the actions caused by ideas or feelings of prejudice. This includes making distinctions between people and placing them into categories considered to be inferior or superior to others based on a visible difference, disregarding their personal qualities.

A person can suffer discrimination based on the color of their skin, country of origin, religion, physical appearance, disabilities, age, gender, sexual orientation, or any apparent difference from the people who choose to discriminate against them. We will look into the discrimination that tries to separate a person from their fundamental human rights and isolates them from interacting and associating with others in their communities.

Racism

Racism encompasses feelings of prejudice and acts of discrimination that are fueled by the idea that human beings are divided into races, and that one race is inferior to another. This wrong idea can lead to dangerous attitudes in people who are willing to harm and even kill those who they consider as inferior.

Racism can also prevent people from having access to opportunities, holding them back from developing their abilities and talents that could be beneficial to others in society. Unfortunately, encountering racism seems unavoidable.

YOUR THOUGHTS ARE WHAT LEAD YOU TO TAKE ACTION.

Our thoughts and the decisions we make today will shape our futures and those of future generations. Indeed, we cannot control what other people think, but we can individually decide what to think and how to react. We have the freedom to choose what we will do in each situation to solve the problems we face and not make them worse.

An important idea to consider is that discrimination and racism are learned behaviors. And in the same way that people learn to be racist, they can also learn to be tolerant and understanding.

Children Are Not Born Racist

When children are born they are pure, and among the little ones there is no racism. In adults however, we witness aggression and racist comments. Compare that attitude to the one of a small child. A little child observes, looks for answers, and is honest when it comes to expressing how they feel and what they think. They are continually looking for information, as simple as it may be, and most of the time, they see the best in people and the situations around them. However, if they are raised exposed to racist experiences, a child can grow up learning to discriminate against others.

We can find many examples in the news and online of children that see themselves as identical to their friends who are different from them in their appearance. These children do not seem to care about exterior differences when making a sincere connection with their friends.

When we look at the behavior of little children, we see that racism and discrimination are taught as we grow up and that we have much to learn from their sincerity. We all must be like a child in this regard. Jesus once said that we must be like children, and whoever is not like a child will not enter the kingdom of heaven (Matthew 18:3), which means they will not experience peace, joy, and fulfillment, but bitterness instead.

My Experiences Growing Up

I want to speak to those who have suffered discrimination. Have you ever been discriminated against?

I was. Have you experienced prejudice? I have experienced a great deal of it. Have you ever been humiliated because of your skin tone? I have. Was your character defined by the color of your skin? This also happened to me; I was wrongfully judged just for being Black. However, I have overcome this within me. Today, others' words do not affect me on the inside, but in the past, everything that people said or did would cause me sadness, anger, and anguish.

When I was a child in school, I suffered from my classmates' prejudice. I experienced racism even from my teachers, many of whom made indirect remarks and showed behaviors that encouraged discrimination. When there is separation, when we divide, it can result in discrimination.

When you do not know your rights, you cannot fight for them. As a child and teenager, I did not know better so I accepted and kept inside of me all the bitterness and pain from the rejection I felt.

I remember a party at school at the end of the year when I was young. The teacher was giving out snacks, and sitting next to me was a White child.

The teacher gave that child a snack and skipped me. In the classroom, teachers prioritized students with lighter skin tones, children that looked like them, and they would leave the Black children aside.

But discrimination was not expressed in words; it was in gestures, in attitudes, hurting even more than words. All forms of discrimination, including racism, are visible.

When a person is empty of the Word of God and lacking understanding of His Word, discrimination can enter their soul and make them feel as if they are the worst person on Earth.

Today discrimination no longer enters my soul; it does not have power over me. Today when people discriminate against me or when they try to belittle me and put me down, my reaction towards them is the same reaction Jesus had on the cross when He was being condemned and spit on. He said, "Father, forgive them, for they do not know what they do" (Luke 23:34).

And I move forward. Their behaviors do not hinder me, and I stand up for my rights. I have overcome it within me, and so can you. Here I will show you step by step how you can achieve this strength and reshape your life despite any prejudice and discrimination.

Will Discrimination Always Exist?

From having a conversation to entering a store, while applying for a job or working to achieve our dreams, we will all eventually face discrimination in our lifetimes. Some will face it more often than others, depending on the circumstances. However, as long as there are interactions between people, there will be some kind of discrimination.

Although discriminating acts that deprive you of your fundamental human and lawful rights are a crime, thoughts of prejudice remain in the minds of people who nurture these feelings. We cannot control what or how they think, yet they have to abide by the law, and we must resort to the law to keep them in check. We can make sure that we do not allow outside voices to change us for worse or limit our abilities.

We cannot control what happens in the world. Will the world change? No, it will not. I cannot say that one day racism and prejudice will end. I cannot change the world, but I can change my life in this world. I cannot end racism and prejudice, but I can change my life regardless of racism and prejudice, and so can you!

Reactions

Our words express our thoughts. They give us insight into what is deep inside of us. So, it is inevitable that words are also used to express feelings of prejudice and racism. These include name-calling, racial slurs, pejorative nicknames, and the list goes on. It all comes down to people using words to express what they think.

When someone calls you names, humiliates you, gives you pejorative nicknames, or puts you down because of the color of your skin, a physical trait, or any other reason, do not draw back, but instead move forward and move ahead with your goals. These words can hurt emotionally, but they do not have the power to stop you. They cannot block you from moving forward. You can succeed!

If you allow criticism, prejudice, or racism to dwell inside of you, you are lost, completely lost. If you accept the mindset of a victim, it will destroy you. From the moment you accept the lower standards laid out for you, then you are belittling and holding yourself back. From the moment you begin to consider yourself inferior or at a disadvantage, you are bound to look for others to blame, and you lose power over your future. Since the responsibility is no longer yours, you will stop pushing forward and lose hope and the purpose for fighting for a better life.

Do not depend on what others think of you. Do not make any stop during your journey to listen to empty and irrational talk. When faced with prejudiced talk, speak to yourself, tell your mind that you are able to overcome that, that you can make it, and move on.

If you have been wrongfully judged based on the color of your skin, your appearance, or discriminated against for any other reason, do not engage in an argument. First of all, you are protected by the law; racism is a crime. Secondly, arguing with others will not change anything: your skin tone will continue to be the same, as will your features, regardless of what they may say. Whether they speak ill or well of you, that does not change who you are. So, do not let what people say about you guide your thoughts and actions.

My advice to you is to not react outspokenly to racial slurs or any other derogatory talk, but neither should you accept these "labels." When you accept these slurs, you put yourself down. The biggest problem is when you agree to be called by slurs and pejorative nicknames. You should not acknowledge them because that is not who you are; it does not represent you. If you bow down to name-calling, you will lose the quality and essence of who you are.

You are a creature of God, created in His image and likeness. Do not allow anyone to change your identity in any way, and do not allow yourself to be known by a nickname or racial slur. From the moment you begin to accept yourself with these hurtful comments, you will enable them to enter and take root in your thoughts. By doing so, these comments will eventually become your reality and will limit your life.

When facing situations like these, you should not draw back and feel downcast. Instead, you must say to yourself, "Now is my time, I will get there. I will prove to myself and to everyone else that I can become a well-known architect, doctor, judge, lawyer... a successful person in all areas of my life regardless of the color of my skin, origin, background, or any visible difference."

Quarreling, insulting, shouting, name-calling, or cursing in response to racism or discrimination will not change anything. Do not argue because it will not improve the situation. In reality, it might make things worse by stirring more anger and violence. Do not fight with your hands or with your words. The more you argue, the worse the situation can get. When you fight physically or verbally, you are bringing yourself to the lower level. Instead, resort to the law that protects you.

I CANNOT CHANGE THE WORLD, BUT I CAN CHANGE MY LIFE IN THIS WORLD.

Exercise Your Rights

We have seen that many people throughout the world do not know their rights, and they put themselves down. They underestimate themselves when they hear hurtful words. When suffering racism, they draw back and become emotionally shaken.

If you suffer racism, there are authorities and the law to protect you, domestically and internationally.

In the Bible, there is the case of the unjust imprisonment of the apostle Paul, for whom God opened the cell and prison to allow him to walk free, but Paul refused. When he was first detained, Paul was humiliated and beaten in public. When the authorities found out that he was a rightful Roman citizen, they asked him to leave in secret (Acts 16:35-40).

However, the apostle Paul did not agree to leave quietly in secret. He sent a message to the authorities to come personally and set him free through the front door. They publicly humiliated him, so publicly, they should acknowledge his rights.

The apostle Paul then walked through the front door because he knew his rights. If you do not know your rights, you will always suffer at the hands of other people. If you are not aware of your rights, you will often belittle yourself and accept less than what is rightfully yours, and even with qualifications and hard work, you will be given less opportunity.

When the apostle Paul left through the front door, other doors were opened to him. God chose him because He saw that Paul was a courageous man that knew his rights. Do not look back and do not blame others, you can make it! You can succeed! Seek the law; make use of your rights. If you suffer a racist crime, you must seek justice under the law.

If you are a Christian, do not think that your belief means that you should allow people to step on you as if you were a doormat. If you pray or go to a church or temple but do not claim your lawful rights, then you are not worthy of them.

The apostle Paul knew his rights, and he did not accept to be humiliated in that way and leave secretly through the back door. He fought for his rights. I am not saying that you ought to fight physically, engage in riots, or be aggressive, no. You should stand up for yourself and fight using the law.

IF YOU PRAY
BUT DO
NOT CLAIM
YOUR LAWFUL
RIGHTS,
THEN YOU
ARE NOT WORTHY
OF THEM.

Do Not Use the Strength of Your Arms

The use of physical violence to fight for one's rights is a way to lose them. Use the correct mediums, for the law is on your side. You have the authorities, communications, and media, like the press, and other intelligent tools that are available today that many people did not have in the past. Go ahead and defend your rights legally.

Remember: we cannot solve one problem by creating another. Many people are doing this and making matters worse day by day.

Racism permeates the entire world. Some people, in an effort to solve this problem, have created other problems—such as violence and aggressive protests—in order to attract the attention of the authorities. However, after the smoke has cleared and when the riots are over, I ask you, doesn't everything stay the same? What changes?

That moment of anger, violence, and protests ends up being forgotten, and things turn out being worse than before. Therefore, we do not solve a problem by creating another one. I would argue that complaining, engaging in violent protests, fighting, and quarreling is a waste of time. Many have done this and died without solving the problem.

We cannot fight using the strength of our arms; we must fight using the strength of our minds: our intelligence. Our hands, arms, and physical strength do not think. We use our brains to think. Every problem has a root; therefore, we must use our intelligence not only to find the causes of each problem but to find and work out the solutions. Attacking other people and using violence does not solve the issues at hand; it just makes the problems worse.

You are intelligent! Use the strength of your mind and not the strength of your arms, for it will not solve anything. Fight for your rights by using the law and communication tools to voice the issue.

However, bear in mind that even though you fight for your rights legally and voice your story, discrimination and racism will still exist because we cannot control what people think and feel. The best way to respond to situations of prejudice and discrimination is to succeed in life. The best answer to humiliation is to be an achiever.

When you face discrimination or racism, I advise you to overcome the obstacles. Where no one else succeeds, you should succeed and strive to achieve where no one does. This is the only way to truly overcome racism.

Perhaps, until now, those who have discriminated against you have looked down on you, they see you as low. But when you overcome the odds, succeed, and go to the top, people have to raise their heads to look at you, where you are now in a higher position with a transformed life. When everyone says "no," when no one believes or trusts in you, but you still move up, you reach another level. People will have to look up and acknowledge you and your God. If they do not respect the color of your skin, they will respect your success. That is how you win. You must overcome, achieve, and succeed, and that will be your response to people who are prejudiced against you.

The best way to overcome racism and prejudice is to do so from within. Never allow anyone to put you down. Racism, prejudice, and discrimination can be solved with positive results when approached through true faith, the faith of Abraham. Many have heard about Abraham because he was a man who believed in the promise of God and in himself (Genesis 12:1-9). He was considered as weak and inferior by others, as this was a time when having descendants was an honor, and a person without children was considered to be cursed. However, he put his faith and trust in God and succeeded in every way, becoming the father of many nations and respected by all. The same can happen to you; God wants to transform the humiliation you have been going through into victory and honor.

When you leave home in the morning, I encourage you to direct your prayers to God, ask for His guidance, and always say to yourself, "I can! I can!" As it is written, "I can do all things through Christ who strengthens me" (Philippians 4:13).

Do not let what others think and say define who you are. God created you to be an overcomer. He gave you abilities and talents. Jesus believes in you. So do not bow down to prejudiced words directed to you or dwelling in your mind. Believe and invest in yourself. Move forward and move up.

Mental Slavery

I ask you, dear reader: What is the difference between the two men depicted in the images shown here? Perhaps you answer that one man is chained and the other one is free. However, I can say that both have chains. Let me explain.

The first image shows a slave in chains, while the second shows a man that is apparently free, but you can notice in his expression that he is also in chains. He is not physically chained, but he is chained in his mind because he carries within himself the following thought: "I can't. This is not for me. I cannot achieve this or that."

Perhaps this has happened to you. You are convinced that you are inferior compared to others. When facing challenges, you put yourself down and end up behaving in a shy and insecure way.

SOS Self-Discrimination

Did you know that one of the worst forms of discrimination is self-discrimination? Discrimination is something imposed on you by external circumstances, while self-discrimination happens inside you, affecting, in turn, your relationship with the outside world. We can block words coming from others, but we cannot do the same to those originating from our minds, which is where our biggest problems are.

Take a look at the following image and think about what you see.

Do you identify with this image? Perhaps you are not in a physical prison, yet in your mind you have become a prisoner of prejudice, your own self-prejudice, and not discrimination from others.

One example that is very close to home for me is when people discriminate against themselves based on the color of their skin. This is something I experienced growing up, and later witnessed and spoke about to hundreds of Blacks experiencing these same thoughts and feelings.

Some people say, "I cannot do anything." They have been raised with this mindset. Some think, "I cannot achieve my dream because I am Black." Others say the following to themselves: "I lack education because I am poor." "I cannot have a successful career because I am an ex-offender." "I cannot have a blessed and happy marriage because of my past."

I want to direct my message to everyone, regardless of skin tone, origin or background: When you leave the house to go to work, perhaps you leave 50% defeated already. By the time you get there, you collapse; you have defeated yourself. Or you go to school thinking you are the worst, and you sit way in the back, avoiding the first rows.

You go to the clinic, and when you arrive, you see there are many other patients like you. However, when you see people that you consider being superior, you hide and sit in the back. Why? You do this because you are a slave in your mind.

Nowadays, Blacks are free from the racial segregation and slavery of the past. There are laws that defend us from discrimination in the workplace, school, and other situations. However, if racism comes from inside a person, if they carry prejudice and the spirit of self-discrimination, then they are enslaved within, even though they are apparently free on the outside.

We have said that the worst kind of discrimination is self-discrimination. But even worse is when people that carry this burden convey these ideas to their children. How many children have said, "We can't go to this school because we are Black?" And how many have said, "I can't dream big and be successful because I am poor and from a small town?"

Many are the children that compare their physical characteristics, financial means, and social status to others. Many inherited these attitudes from their parents, who were full of self-discrimination. Unfortunately, this way of thinking will continue to be passed on to future generations.

Perhaps you can identify with this attitude. You draw back because of the feeling of inferiority inside you. Even though you are strong, you see yourself as weak; even though you are intelligent and capable, you see yourself without abilities or value. When adverse situations have happened around you, do you become shy, full of grudges and regrets, and feel as if you were stuck in a dead end? Set yourself free within! Free yourself from prejudice and the spirit of self-discrimination that you have been carrying inside.

Freedom and Victory

True freedom does not occur solely on the outside and around us; it is something that occurs mainly inside of us, in our minds. I am convinced that the external aspects of your life are a consequence of what you have inside. When you are free within, external circumstances cannot imprison you. People might want to humiliate you, but because you are free inside, this freedom will influence other aspects of your life and your surroundings as well.

Happiness and achievement do not depend on the color of your skin, your background, or any outside distinction. What truly makes the difference resides inside of you, in your mind. Your life is a reflection of your thoughts.

If you are defeated in your mind, you will be defeated on the outside as well. However, if you are victorious inside, you will overcome any situation regardless of any prejudice coming from others, and you will achieve your goals and succeed, wherever you may be.

Years ago, I was counseling a young lady who had a job as a housekeeper. We talked about how she had a decent job, but I also tried to explain the importance of investing in her future.

"You make a living as a housekeeper, but you will get older and won't be able to bend and move around as easily in the way that is required for your job. Your body will not be able to bear the same physical efforts it does today. You must invest in your future, like taking courses or learning a new career that you will be able to perform for many years so that you may advance. God wants you to advance. And you can!" I told her.

When I finished speaking, she replied, "My problem is here (pointing to her head), I can't learn. When I go to school, I cannot understand what the teacher says. I cannot read properly. I am not good at school. I am not able to do it, and I can't understand why this happens to me."

I then pointed to her head and said that her problem was indeed there, and I continued to explain: "It is not a learning problem, because you are an intelligent being. However, by what you said, you are not using your intelligence because you continuously say, 'I can't, I can't learn, I can't understand what the teacher says…'"

This young lady felt sad because she was having a hard time learning, but this was not the problem. The main problem was that she entered the classroom assuming that she was not going to learn, that she was not able. With this mindset, you only put yourself down, and even the easiest of things can become difficult.

Perhaps, dear reader, you also say the same things: "I can't read, I can't have ideas, I am not intelligent, I am not qualified..." Nevertheless, I assure you that this is not true. It could have been that a bad experience drove you to think this way and bound you to these mental chains. However, these hurtful thoughts are not the truth about you. Stop telling yourself that you can't make it. Instead, believe that you can succeed!

Another example took place in South Africa, where I lived for six years working in the community there. One lady shared a sad story with us. She told us of how she had applied for a job at a big company in Johannesburg. She was called in for an interview, as she was qualified for the position. She prepared, put together her resume and went to the interview. When she arrived, she realized that there were only *umlungus* present—the word Blacks in South Africa use to refer to Whites—.

Many Blacks would say, "This car is for *umlungus*," "This house is for *umlungus*," or "This movie theater is for *umlungus*." Perhaps you think this way and say, "No, this is for White people," or worse, "This is for people who are more 'beautiful.'"

Who told you that you are ugly? I don't see myself as ugly! It is your mind that has been saying this because of the experiences of discrimination you have had in the past.

Going back to the story, when this lady saw that there were many White people, she took the folder with her resume and went home. The following day, the manager of the company called her and said, "We waited for you yesterday. Why did you miss the interview? I want to say that of all the candidates we interviewed, you were the most qualified." She lost an opportunity because she was a slave in her mind. It is clear that the manager of the company was not concerned about the color of her skin; the manager only considered her resume, qualifications, talents, and potential.

Here in the United States, someone did the opposite when all odds were against her. I am talking about Rosa Parks. Despite having the law at the time against her, she did not place herself in the last place, but instead stood her ground, believing in her worth, her value as a human being and a soul. Parks was detained when she claimed her place in the front seats of the bus, but her attitude opened doors for a positive change.

There is a place up front for you, so do not sit in the back. You might lower yourself at school or at work because you are not aware of the value and the power that you have inside. Never accept to be enslaved by these thoughts of self-discrimination or by the outright prejudice of others against you.

Perhaps you have suffered discrimination at school, at work, and in your social life. Some people might have even not considered you to be a human being. You are carrying the emotional and physical scars of racism, discrimination, humiliation, shame, anguish, and suffering. Perhaps you have been humiliated in front of others, and people laughed at you, making you feel isolated and lonely. Or maybe your story has been of failed marriages and betrayal, of failed businesses, of dreams that turned into nightmares, and you have been chained by these experiences ever since. You can change your story.

How to Be Free Within

True freedom comes from within and is not dependent on your circumstances in life. When you are free from the chains of mental slavery, external conditions cannot imprison you. If you are victorious in your mind, then you will overcome, achieve, and succeed in life.

The transformation, the result, and the answers begin within you. Your thoughts are more powerful than you can imagine. Every decision you make starts with your thoughts. The thoughts that you have accepted as your truths determine your actions, reactions, and—believe it or not—they also shape your future.

To change the way you act, you must first change the way you think. By changing your thoughts, you will change your life, without a doubt. Your life will never change as long as you keep thinking the same. For you to have a new life, old thoughts need to end. Throw away all those thoughts from the past. Forget them.

Let go of ideas such as: "My father suffered discrimination and did not succeed in life. The same will happen to me." "My mother did not have a family, and now I have a broken family." "People like me can't dream big." "People like me don't have opportunities." "No one in my family made it far in life. Why should I be any different?"

No! Remove these thoughts from your mind!

But you may ask, "How can I get rid of these thoughts when they have been there for so long, perhaps for generations?" There is a tool capable of helping you see beyond appearances, and that is FAITH. The light brought on by faith enables you to see opportunities amid chaos, and hope in the face of adversity. In the next chapter you will learn more about this powerful tool that can change your life from the inside out.

When the Light of Faith shines on you, your face will light up like Moses' face did, and your life will shine as well (Exodus 34:29). Your eyes will sparkle, and your face will reflect what is inside you. No one will look at you as a slave, but as someone who has a special radiance, which is the Light of God that will help you overcome this complex issue inside you.

Begin by saying, "I can!" Do not self-discriminate but place yourself in the first place on the podium.

You have it within you.

TRUE FREEDOM BEGINS MAINLY WITHIN OUR MINDS.

Take time to identify the words you have spoken and the thoughts of self-discrimination that have been plaguing you and decide that from now on you will not live according to them, and never again repeat them to yourself.

You will speak to yourself in different terms from now on: "I can! I am capable! I will achieve!" The Lord Jesus says to you, "You can!"

Set yourself free from the mental slavery that has held you back for so many years.

Write down the steps of change you will need to take starting now.

FAITH HAS NO COLOR

The Greatest Tool to Overcome Discrimination and Racism

The Creator of all things has never differentiated people by the color of their skin. God sees us all the same; and He granted to each one of us the same measure of faith, regardless of skin-tone or any other physical trait or background. God is not interested in gender, race, how you look, if you can speak well or not, or anything of the sort. God only differentiates between people based on their faith put into practice. We find evidence of it in the story of Rahab, who was a foreigner and also a prostitute. However, through her faith, God transformed her life, gave her a family and the privilege of being part of the genealogy of Jesus Christ (Joshua 2; Matthew 1). This same faith turned an enslaved man in Egypt into the highest authority in the land under the Pharaoh

(Genesis 41); and Joseph's faith led him to victory even amid extreme adversity.

You might ask, "What is this faith? Is it religion?" No, intelligent faith is NOT religion. Faith is certainty in what we cannot see (Hebrews 11:1), assurance of God's existence, His purpose for us, certainty in His justice and love, and in the truth and wisdom of His Word. This faith overcomes all doubts.

Your faith does not have color; it is a force that helps you move ahead; it encourages you to make efforts and persevere. It guides you to succeed and achieve. It is a power inside of you.

If you have an active faith in God, any discrimination that happened in the past, which exists nowadays and will take place in the future, will not affect you because you have a living faith in God inside of you.

What Is Intelligent Faith?

Intelligent faith is the faith that helps us think and act according to God's Word. It is not based on what we feel or see. It is shaped by our trust in His Word. Intelligent faith does not need to see to believe, and it does not need to feel a certain way. It disregards the information our senses provide, and it moves us based on God's promises. Emotions do not sway it because it allows us to see beyond and envision the bigger picture.

One example from the Bible that comes to mind is that of Joshua. The people of Israel did not know how to overcome the barriers that prevented them from entering the Promised Land. God, seeing their difficulty, spoke to Joshua and told him that He had delivered Jericho into his hands. Still, Joshua had not yet taken possession of what God had determined: the physical barriers were in the same place, and the limitations remained the same to human eyes. However, let's see how Joshua reacted to that promise:

> "And Joshua said to the people, 'Sanctify yourselves, for tomorrow the Lord will do wonders among you.'"
> (Joshua 3:5)

He heard, believed, and acted on the voice of God. As a result, the walls that seemed indestructible fell before him. If we hear, believe, and act on what God has determined in His Word, so it shall be done, regardless of the circumstances.

Intelligent faith does not have loopholes or shortcuts, and it is not hypocritical. It is pure, sincere, and leaves absolutely no room for doubt. Many are those who have confused their emotions with faith, seeking shortcuts in religions and traditions with no real outcomes. The reality for many is that their faith does not match the thoughts of God nor His intentions. Instead, they solely want to feel, touch and see to believe and trust.

It is not enough to say that you have intelligent faith; you must put it into practice. When we take an action that pleases God, the barriers and walls of prejudice will fall. What you want to achieve depends solely on the actions driven by your intelligent faith.

Many people feel that they are always struggling, striving, and overworking without achieving anything. Instead, they deal with and tolerate daily frustrations and failures. However, once the flame of an intelligent faith empowers them, they find the strength to achieve what they have aspired.

Intelligent faith will help you overcome and succeed even when no one believes in you. That is what happened to Joseph, whose story is mentioned in the Bible. He was sold as a slave and went to jail and later walked free and succeeded in life.

There is no other way for a person to be blessed and overcome racism and prejudice except living in active faith. Intelligent faith is the only tool that can help people reach the benefits promised by God.

Do not feel sorry for yourself because of the struggles you have faced, whether this is prejudice, financial difficulties, or any other injustice against you. These feelings will never change your life, nor will they take you to the next level. Instead, raise your head and begin using an intelligent faith.

Without actions of faith nothing will be done for you. Don't expect pity from others.

What happens when someone trips and falls? If they remain on the floor, they will surely die.

But instead, they get up and keep going. When we use our intelligent faith, we get up after any setback, from adverse situations, and we move ahead.

> *"I can do all things through Christ who strengthens me."*
> *(Philippians 4:13)*

You can always say, "I can," even when being wrongfully judged due to racism and even when others look down on you based on your appearance or incorrect information. But you judge yourself through the faith you carry within. Yes, you can!

You can become a successful woman and a loved wife. You can become a respected husband and a family man because it will NOT be the color of your skin, your origin, physical characteristics and abilities, or your background that will keep you from succeeding.

What you have inside of you is what leads you to victory or defeat. Your intelligent faith will bring you inner peace. In the face of adversity, it will keep you standing and will help you.

IT IS NOT ENOUGH TO SAY THAT YOU HAVE AN INTELLIGENT FAITH; YOU MUST PUT IT INTO PRACTICE.

Intelligent Faith Leads to Freedom

I want to show you something very important. Please read the following carefully:

> *"Now the Lord is the Spirit; and where the Spirit of the Lord is, there is liberty."*
> *(2 Corinthians 3:17)*

God is Spirit. He is not an emotion. He is not a human being and cannot be swayed by feelings, appearances, or mere words. He knows our soul and most inner thoughts.

God is not a physical being limited by space and time, human hands, or any other circumstance. He is Spirit, and where the Spirit of God is, there is freedom. When He enters a person's life, depression dissipates. Anguish, negative thoughts, suicidal thoughts, weakness... it all goes away. Why? Because there is freedom wherever the Spirit of God is.

This helps you build the strength to say, "I can," and leave behind any negative thoughts about your situation. Through the Spirit of God, which is the Spirit of Faith, you then begin to say, "I can."

How to Overcome Prejudice Through Intelligent Faith?

If God is the source of justice, love, and faith, we can only conclude that injustice does not come from Him. Every injustice, suffering, problem, or struggle does not come from God because He cannot deny Himself. Human beings are unfair and unjust. God is not unfair or unjust; He is not a monster. He is justice and cannot be any other way. God wants you to lead a righteous life.

They say that justice is blind. This saying is true. Human justice is blind, but God's justice is not blind. God sees your situation.

Jesus once taught the parable of a widow who had nobody to defend her. In those days, people used to take advantage of widows because they knew that her husband had passed away, meaning that she was alone. This widow went to a judge asking him to hear her case, and to make the situation worse, the judge was unfair. He was unjust and refused to rule in her favor and grant what was rightfully hers.

If the person holding the authority to execute the law was unfair, can you imagine those under him? However, thanks to her insistence, she achieved the result she wanted, despite an unjust judge.

Jesus says, "And shall God not avenge His own elect who cry out day and night to Him…?" (Luke 18:7) You know, you can go straight to God. You have free and direct access to Him. You do not need to depend on a pastor, a bishop, a deacon, or a priest to pray. You don't need anybody to intercede for you because He hears your voice when you cry out to Him.

God is the source of justice, and when you approach Him with sincere faith, He never fails. We can bring our burdens to Him, for God is willing to help us. He is the only One capable of doing justice in our lives. All He needs is to witness our faith.

If you are among those who refuse to accept injustice as the norm, Jesus tells you, "Resist the devil and he will flee from you" (James 4:7).

Racism and discrimination, for example, are tools that Evil uses to kill, steal, and destroy (John 10:10). We see people fighting against each other for reasons of skin color or origins, but the problem is mainly a spiritual one. We can learn from Jesus Himself how to fight this injustice. In the desert, He overcame Evil through the Word of God.

He said, "It is written…" (Matthew 4:4)

Whenever you have thoughts of self-doubt, self-discrimination, anger, grudges, frustration, of giving up or committing a terrible mistake, you must go to the Word of God to resist these thoughts.

If you do not fight Evil, you will never be free. You must resist it with all your power, with all your might. How? By meditating and practicing the Word of God, which is the fuel for an intelligent faith.

Only through the Word of God can we overcome harmful thoughts and bad feelings. There is no other way for a person to be blessed and overcome racism and prejudice.

The Word of God is above any other, and it has the power to transform you and restore your life. If what you need and want is a new beginning, a fresh start, the Word of God does it all.

Jesus said that those who come to Him would never be driven away (John 6:37). If you come to God and place your trust in His Word, He will not turn away, regardless of your past or any other reason why people have judged you before.

I tell you: Read and meditate in the Bible. I am not trying to teach you to be religious. When I say read the Bible, I mean for you to do it in preparation to face and overcome unhealthy thoughts, doubts, feelings of falling back, of giving up and doing the same things over and over. When you read the Bible, you nourish your spirit and make yourself ready.

When tempted by His enemy, Jesus said, "It is written, 'Man shall not live by bread alone, but by every word that proceeds from the mouth of God'" (Matthew 4:4).

By meditating on God's Word and applying it into your life, you will overcome all fears, doubts, and negative and suicidal thoughts because you will be equipped with the Word of God. This not only sets you free from all self-discrimination, but it guides you towards a happy and fulfilling life.

Recall Joseph's story now, whose life wasn't good and who was likely destined to live miserably and die in poverty. He had a dream, but his brothers tried to kill him out of envy. Remember, when you have an idea, a project, do not share it with anybody too soon. Learn to keep it to yourself. Joseph spoke too much, stirring his brothers' envy and feelings of killing him. But instead, they sold him as a slave.

God does not want you to be a slave. God does not call you to be anyone's slave. So, when you have faith in the Word of God, even though others might try to stop you, that will not be possible. Though they might try to block you and mess up your life, they can't.

Wherever Joseph went, he became a leader. He was first sold as a slave and taken to the captain's house in Egypt. After some time, he became the leader of the house (Genesis 39). Later, he was put in jail unjustly, but there he became the prisoners' leader, and the jail keeper trusted him. When you have the blessing of God upon you, nobody can stop you.

THE WORD OF GOD IS ABOVE ANY OTHER, AND IT HAS THE POWER TO TRANSFORM YOUR LIFE.

Who is above or stronger than God? No one. That is why we do not fight physically or verbally because it is a waste of time.

Do not fight against those who oppress you by yelling at them, cursing or any form of aggression. Instead show the world your results, because they speak louder than empty words. Stop talking and show everyone who your God is.

When in God we do not lose. Just like Joseph, who was imprisoned unjustly yet became a leader, you can be a leader wherever you go as well. Joseph believed in the promise of God. Eventually, he became the governor. His brothers saw it, the inmates in prison saw it, and the Pharaoh and everybody in Egypt respected him. When you believe in God, and you believe in yourself, no one can stop you.

> "With men this is impossible, but with
> God all things are possible."
> (Matthew 19:26)

People respect you not for what you say but for what you do. God wants to make the impossible happen in your life. Everyone around you will see the power of your faith through the results in your life.

Your Fifty Percent

Faith can be compared to a pillar. If a pillar falls, the entire house or building it supports will tumble as well. If your faith breaks, so will your family, marriage, career, and every other area of your life.

Faith brings your life up, and doubt puts you down. Many have been bound by their problems because of doubt. You want to believe that your life can change, but you doubt that it can because of your overwhelming troubles.

When in doubt, do not make any major decisions. Stop, pray to God, and ask for His guidance. Doubt can make you take a wrong turn. Doubts, unlike faith, produce defeat.

You need to keep your faith standing and secure against any doubts. When doubts are strong, your faith will surely be weak. You keep your faith high by:

1. Speaking to God in prayer,
2. Listening to Him speak through His Word, and
3. Taking actions of obedience to His will.

These three steps of intelligent faith will keep it strong and active and you will remain standing regardless of whatever injustices come your way.

"What do you want Me to do for you?" asks Jesus (Luke 18:41). What do you want God to do for you?

Someone might say, "Why should we speak to God? Doesn't He already know the situations we are facing?" Yes, God knows all things, but to see Him in our lives we must invite Him in, and we must go to Him. This is a crucial step of faith.

Prayer is not about kneeling and praying and praying and praying. God does not hear nor is looking for beautiful and eloquent words. What God wants to hear is your sincerity.

When you pray to God, you must be sincere. God values truth and sincerity. He is merciful, but He is also just. We must pray according to what is righteous. We cannot ask Him to go against His

Word, but we can rest assured that He will fulfill all He has promised. Be bold and invoke the name of Jesus, as He paid the price to give us a fresh new start and bring us closer to God (Galatians 3:13-14, Matthew 27).

God does not merely improve your life—He transforms it. Whenever you receive "leftovers," they do not come from God. It is Evil that wants to blind you with petty things for you to become dependent and remain where you are.

When Jesus turned water into wine at the wedding, He did not make the water better; He offered the best wine (John 2:10). When you pray, remember to say, "God, you changed water. I have more value to You than water. You changed the water; You can transform my life."

The second step is to listen carefully to what God has to say. His answers are not always pleasing, but they challenge you to change for the better. When you meditate in God's Word you must be humble.

The third step is to take action. Many people pray, and even learn from the Bible, thinking about the issues they have to solve, but they do not take action. They say, "I place it in God's hands."

I must be honest: prayers alone will not help you. Prayers are not enough. Do not say that you have placed the issue in God's hands. God has given you the faith to take action. No matter how big or small your problems may be, you have to fight to overcome them. Your problems will not go away by only leaving them in God's hands. Perhaps you have been complacent and say, "God will make a way." Yes, He makes a way when we take the first step. Upon taking the first step, He will make a way.

God reacts when we act. There may be times when you have thought that God didn't care, that He was not there for you. But in reality, God does care. However, He is waiting for your actions. When you take action, God does what you cannot do.

Moses, one of the greatest heroes of faith in the Bible, had in front of him the Red Sea, with the Egyptians behind him and the children of Israel. He had his rod with him and prayed asking God to do something. Then God said to Moses, "Why do you cry to Me? Tell the children of Israel to go forward" (Exodus 14:15). Moses followed God's command, directed his rod towards the sea, and the miracle happened, the sea parted, and the children of Israel moved ahead.

There are some things that are only for God to do, but there are other things that we must do for ourselves. We have to take action. Maybe someone has been speaking ill about you in your workplace, and you pray, "God, reveal the truth." But you have all the evidence needed to prove that the person is lying. You have to go to your manager or boss and inform them of what is happening. If they believe you or not, that is something else, but you have done your part. You have taken the first step.

So now you have prayed and placed your situation in God's hands, and now God has given you the conditions for you to make a decision. Perhaps it is just a phone call you need to make to deal with the matter. Maybe after filling out an application, you continue waiting for an answer that never comes, yet you pray and pray, even going to church or temple, while saying to yourself, "I have placed it in God's hands."

You have to realize that God has placed it in your hands, so do not keep waiting. Go there and say, "Do I have an answer? You promised after the interview to call me, and I have not received anything." There is nothing wrong with doing so.

A lady once told me that she applied for her immigration papers. She needed a visa, and she waited and waited. One day, she decided to go to the immigration authorities to find out the status of her application. She was told, "It's been almost two months since we sent you an approval letter. We thought you didn't want the visa anymore." When she did not receive the letter, instead of taking action, she prayed and kept waiting. Prayer alone will not solve your problems; you must put your faith into practice. Do not expect God to do for you what you are supposed to do. Let us act. Let us move forward.

Faith in God and Faith in Yourself

When referring to the God of the Bible, I am talking about a God that is strong, the only God I know and can mention. Because I believe in Him, I also believe in myself and my potential. I believe in God, but I also am confident that I can accomplish my goals.

I want to address those who feel they are failing in life. I want to show you why you feel this way or consider yourself to be a failure, even when you say that you believe in a great God. Truthfully, that is not enough; you also have to believe in yourself. Perhaps you often say to yourself, "I am not qualified. I don't have the skills. I don't have a good education. That's why I don't succeed." And, when you see others succeeding, you say, "This is not for me. I cannot make it. These people are better than me, that's why they are successful and I am not." When you have these kinds of thoughts in your mind, it shows that you do not believe in yourself.

Can you see God? No, you cannot. He is Spirit. So how can you say that you believe in Him, whom you cannot see, and yet not believe in yourself? You see the reflection of your face every time you look in the mirror. If you do not believe in someone you can see, how can you believe in whom you cannot see?

It is not enough that you *believe* in God; you also have to *believe in yourself.*

Perhaps your life has been pitiful, defeated, and unfruitful because you do not believe in yourself. Imagine a boxer that goes into the ring thinking that they do not have what it takes to win the match. In this mindset, it is better not even to begin the fight. They will go into the ring to be beaten.

Many people face life's battles already defeated because they do not believe in themselves or their potential. My friend, if you do not believe in yourself, then forget about it, no one else will believe in you either. You must say to yourself, "I want, I can, and I will succeed."

Do you know how you should start your day? It is not with your right or left foot. You must wake up with faith in God above everything else, and then faith in yourself. Every day the first thing you should say to yourself is, "I can!" You will live much better on your way to a successful life.

Do not try to be someone you are not. Do not wish to be the same as the next person. It might be that they are not actually happy or as successful as you may think. Happiness and achievement do not depend on external circumstances.

It is time for you to believe in your potential. When you start believing in yourself, God will help you, and your life will begin to move forward. God does not bless those who do not believe in themselves. When you believe in God and yourself, then you are unstoppable!

The Holy Spirit – The Spirit of Faith

The Holy Spirit is God Himself inside of us. God is Spirit, not emotions. Many people believe they have received the Holy Spirit because they felt an overwhelming feeling, in some cases, to the point of losing control of their minds and bodies.

However, the Spirit of God, the Spirit of Faith, gives us the strong ability of self-control. This means that we have power over our actions and reactions; in other words, we become capable of controlling our feelings and making decisions with our intelligent faith.

The Holy Spirit enables us to be guided NOT by what we see or experience but by the Word of God. A person that truly has the Holy Spirit does not pass judgment on appearances and is not controlled by their emotions, but instead has their feelings under control. The Holy Spirit brings permanent joy and happiness as long as that person continues to have a relationship with Him.

This happened to me. My family was in pain. We suffered from illnesses, addictions, and we lived in poverty. I grew up sick as a child and spent more time in the hospital than at home. I had to take many injections because of a chronic disease in my throat.

In her desperation, my mother began to seek help and strength to rescue herself and her family. God saw her faith and guided her to a ministry that taught her how to use the faith she already had; the same faith that drove her not to accept her situation and seek a change in life. She learned about intelligent faith and began putting it to practice.

My family broke free from the chains of sickness, depression, addiction, and poverty. When we were at the bottom of the pit of suffering, Jesus reached out to us and lifted us from that pit. I decided to get baptized, which was a lifelong decision of surrendering my life to Jesus. I saw His power through my healing and the deliverance of my family. But what happened next transformed me completely.

Although I was just a teenager, I was lost and broken inside. When I realized how empty, how lost I was, I had an amazing experience with God, something very spiritual that words cannot explain. He showed me how valuable I am to Him. Jesus began changing my thoughts and character. I did not want to go back to the old ideas and emptiness. I knew that I was going to face problems, prejudice, but I knew I did not want to go back and succumb to these emotions and give up. I learned and understood that I needed the Holy Spirit, the Spirit of Faith, God's power inside of me.

I dedicated my thoughts to seeking the Holy Spirit through my actions and, ultimately, my life. That's when it happened one late night while I was praying and asking God for the Holy Spirit... I remember it as if it were today. I did not feel anything different in my body, I did not see anything unusual, but I knew the exact moment when the Holy Spirit entered my heart. I was filled with immense and indescribable peace. From that moment on, a deep desire to help others was born inside of me, to pass on to others the strength, the joy, and peace I had received: The Holy Spirit.

All my thoughts changed. All the discrimination, the rejection I had suffered based on the color of my skin, all the prejudice I faced, and the hurt it brought, it all disappeared. From then on, I understood my value to God. My character changed completely through the Holy Spirit.

I confess that to this day there are people who judge me based on the color of my skin. I can see it in their gestures and behaviors. But that has no impact on me because those who have the Holy Spirit know that the soul has no color, and they have inner peace regardless of what happens around them. I am secure within me because of the Holy Spirit, regardless of any situation I may face.

The Spirit of God is gentle, yet He is powerful, a strong Spirit. What makes you strong is not your money, job, not even your spouse. What makes you strong is the Holy Spirit, the Spirit of Faith, the Spirit of Power, for He is stronger than you, stronger than your background, society, stereotypes, prejudice, discrimination, and racism... Stronger than anything, everything and anyone!

Many people have been defeated because they do not have the light of the Holy Spirit inside of them. If you feel this way it is because you are going through the same thing. If you do not have the light of the Holy Spirit inside of you, then your interior is shadowed with negative thoughts that have led you to lead a defeated life. Even when opportunities arise, you lose.

Regardless of the circumstances, discrimination, or injustices a person may encounter, if they have the light of the Holy Spirit inside of them, they will overcome, they will win. In your life, no one will continue to look at you as a victim. Your life will shine even in the face of obstacles.

Right now, I say to you, "Receive Light inside of you!" And, the shadows of prejudice and self-discrimination are removed from your life in Jesus' name. Receive the Light of Faith, the Divine Light that will make you shine like the midday sun.

Make a decision today to start from square one and build up your faith. Set time apart to talk to God and meditate on His Word, even if it is new to you. Make it a challenge. Put His Word into practice and invest in seeking and pleasing the Holy Spirit. You will indeed notice the changes inside of you. Write down the daily steps you will take to achieve this.

The Greatest Obstacle to Intelligent Faith

Our emotions are like the waves of the sea, easily moved by the circumstances around us, shaken by the winds of problems, hatred from others, betrayal. Our emotions are influenced by what we hear, see, smell, and touch, by the words and behavior of the people around us. Emotions can be affected by health problems, and even by what we eat. We are continually interacting with our environment, and our emotions are being affected by it. Anything and anyone can help shape our emotions.

We can't necessarily decide what to feel and not to feel; it is a natural part of who we are as human beings. However, we can decide what to think, how to act, and how to react. Emotions have their place and function in our lives, and when out of place, they can become an effective obstacle to intelligent faith.

Emotions and Music

We have a great opportunity in being able to express our feelings and thoughts through music, which is a big part of the human experience. It is a natural part of every culture on our planet. We are musical creatures.

Without a doubt, when listening to a song that we like and which inspires us, we tend to feel pleasure and joy. We have a sense of happiness. The question is, however, are we truly happy? Does this feeling reflect our everyday reality? Does it match the truth that is inside of us?

Many people rely on music or the beautiful songs of the choir to feel good. However, when the music ends, their problems are still there, and they become frustrated and depressed.

Just feeling good is not enough. Although music has a valuable place in our lives, much of it is still influenced and filled with emotions, which can leave us complacent and neutralize the action of our faith. Prejudice will always be there, and problems will always exist, and living by our emotions is not effective when it comes to facing obstacles in life.

We can see that reflected in the lives of some musicians, who receive so much applause but end up losing themselves to depression and drugs. The happiness they feel on stage quickly fades away when facing hardship in life. When facing adversity, music and emotions can only do so much, they cannot transform the situation, and the temporary feeling they bring encourages us to be complacent with our situation.

I have noticed this in the life of many who make music and emotions the foundation of their belief in God. They become frustrated when realizing they have "built their house on the sand" (Matthew 7:26). When facing trials or challenges, they realize they have been led by their emotions and not by faith in the Word of God.

Many are the people that sing beautiful hymns, who feel strong emotions as they sing in church, but when faced with temptations, they do the opposite of what they say they believe.

We see choir singers who are facing depression, problems in their marriages, addictions, and many who are still slaves in their minds (see Chapter 2). Their singing does not reflect the reality of their lives, and it is not able to help them overcome their problems. Intelligent faith teaches us that there is time for everything.

> "To everything there is a season, a time for every purpose under heaven: (...) A time to weep, and a time to laugh; a time to mourn, and a time to dance..."
> (Ecclesiastes 3:1,4)

The Holy Spirit, the Spirit of Faith, gives us understanding and wisdom to decide the right time to sing and dance and when we need to take actions of faith instead. Music and emotions have their place and function in our lives. They express how we feel and help us to keep good memories, to connect with the people we love and the things we hold dear. However, music and emotions, when used at the wrong time, can neutralize our faith. Intelligent faith will require us to take actions that go against what we can see and feel to live according to God's Word and believe in His promises.

When facing injustice and prejudice, music and emotions do not function well. They give you a sense of hope and happiness that quickly fades away when facing reality again. Let music and dance reflect what you are truly living within you. If you are free within, happy and fulfilled, then sing and dance! Use it to express the real peace and joy you have inside of you.

If that is not the case, if you lack this peace, this confidence, this freedom, then fight for it, seek it and put all your strength into building your faith. This is not the time to sing and dance; it is not a time for celebrating, but a time to humble yourself and seek the Holy Spirit with all your mind and heart.

LIVING BY OUR
EMOTIONS
IS NOT
EFFECTIVE
WHEN FACING
CHALLENGES
IN LIFE.

Emotions and Religion

Throughout the years, I have seen and spoken to many believers from various religions and different backgrounds who have lived an emotional faith. Many believe in a great God but have not seen Him in their lives.

Many people attend church, they sing in the choir, they speak the church language, but their life is empty. When you look at their lives, all you see is misery—a picture of defeat. The truth is that this type of faith is an illusion.

If your faith is based on pure emotions, it will not work, regardless of your position or responsibilities in a religious institution. What is faith based on emotions? It is a faith based on what you can see, hear, touch, feel, and smell.

When a person feels a chill down their spine when they pray, they say, "Oh, God is touching me…" When they do not feel anything, they think that God abandoned them. When the song is good, and the melody and lyrics are beautiful, they even cry. However, when they leave the church and face serious problems, they become desperate and cry out of sadness. Why? Because they do not know what to do to solve their problems.

This is the consequence of living an emotional faith: you are shaken by each strong wind that blows (the problems). When the "gust" pushes you far, you go. If it changes direction, you change directions as well. You become a weak person, someone that needs more and more emotional support to feel happy.

> *"For we walk by faith, not by sight."*
> *(2 Corinthians 5:7)*

This is it! It is by faith and not by sight, smell, touch, taste, etc. It is not about what is in front of you; it is about what God can do, which is anything and EVERYTHING. Stop living by emotion, feelings, and awaken your faith. You have a power inside of you capable of changing your life.

Perhaps you know the Bible more than I do. You might have been to Bible studies; but listen, look at your life! Show me your knowledge, and I will show you the result of my life... the result of my faith.

It is like going to a restaurant and reading through the whole menu, but not ordering any food. If you do not order anything, although you know the menu, you will still be hungry, you are still starving, only smelling the food coming from the kitchen.

When a person is religious, they give thanks for everything. They say, "Praise God for my life." However, that does not mean they have a praiseworthy life.

Perhaps you have read your Bible from Genesis to Revelation, from cover to cover. You go to church and say, "I have my home church."

But the reality is that when you look at your life and look at yourself, you realize that you have an incomplete life. You are broken. Your life is the picture of injustice, and you have been a miserable woman, a miserable man. God wants to complete your life.

> "...He who has begun a good work in
> you will complete it..."
> (Philippians 1:6)

I want you to know that God does not work halfway. Many have practiced religion, held religious responsibilities and titles, given advice, and tried to help others. Many have spoken about peace when lacking peace, spoken about love while seeing their families breaking apart. Many have been in church every Sunday morning but have not been able to overcome addictions. God did not call you to live a defeated and incomplete life. God did not call you to live as a slave but to be completely free.

The work of God is complete! He gives you freedom within. He gives you a new mind, a new vision. He gives you control over your emotions. God does not carry out incomplete work. He does not make things better... He transforms!

You can begin a new life! You can start afresh! The Holy Spirit wants to begin transforming your life today, right now. Choose to live by an intelligent faith in the Word of God and not by how you feel.

The Holy Spirit and Emotions

As mentioned in Chapter 3, God is Spirit. And where the Spirit of God is, there is liberty. God is freedom, real freedom for those who place their trust in Him.

The Holy Spirit is not an emotion or a feeling. He is not a chill down the spine or a good sensation that fades away as the circumstances change. The happiness He brings does not depend on positive circumstances, a beautiful song, or praises from others. God sets us free from all dependency on people and things. The person that receives the Holy Spirit becomes a life-giver, no longer depending on anything else to feel better.

Many people feel empty inside because they do not have the Spirit of Faith inside of them. Yet they try to improve themselves on the outside.

Perhaps while you are around others you pretend to be happy, but when you go back home and are alone in your bedroom with the door shut, when you take off the mask and look in the mirror, you see how sad and frustrated you are.

Nowadays, people do not smile; instead, they show their teeth. When taking a picture, a selfie, people tend just to show their teeth.

A prophet mentioned in the Bible was sent to a valley that was full of dry bones, which were spread all over. As instructed by God, he prophesied to those dry bones, which became a vast army of human beings (Ezekiel 37:1-14). However, something was missing: the Spirit.

He prophesied again and the Spirit of God gave life to those "zombies." Without the Holy Spirit, you are like a "zombie"; you are apparently alive, but in reality, you are dead inside, you are without life.

And when people look at you, they can tell that you are always downcast. You look so sad, so pale, and even when you smile, it is a weary and faint smile. All these problems end when the Spirit of God reaches your body. When the Spirit of God enters your soul, you do not need to force things, you do not need to pretend you are happy. The truth is that when you are filled with God (inside), this is reflected in your face (exterior).

Your attitudes, actions, and reactions show who you are and what you have inside of you. Upon hearing bad news, those who do not have the Holy Spirit fall, and they melt like snow in the sun of spring. When they hear bad news, they fight against human beings. They want to fight verbally or physically. Many people are strong in their arms, in their hands, and even in their words. They like to scream and shout and fight verbally and physically. But when you are strong within, and you are strong when you have the Holy Spirit, you do not fight physically. The Lord fights for you because you depend on Him, and you show your strength through your intelligent faith.

I witnessed many testimonies of people who used to be rude, anxious, aggressive, and suicidal, whose past would follow them wherever they would go. However, today, they are free and different. Why? Because they received and preserved the Light of God, the Holy Spirit, within themselves.

You do not have to live your life trying to pretend. The truth is that you are not able to fake it even if you wanted to because your face shows what is inside of you. When you seek and receive the Holy Spirit, your face will show the Light that is inside of you, and your life will change completely.

> *"I will give of the fountain of the water of life freely to him who thirsts."*
> (Revelation 21:6)

Take a look at the picture below:

When the water falls, it does so with power. Imagine somebody who has behaved badly, has a bad reputation, and this person is under this falling water. Now imagine that this water comes from the fountain of God, washing away all your past, your sorrows, traumas, bad behavior, ugly thoughts and feelings, and transforms you into a different person.

The Holy Spirit changes your mentality, your behavior and your nature. He makes you into a different person. All the Holy Spirit needs is for you to empty yourself, which means letting go of religiosity, emotional faith, and pride. Listen to His voice now and let go of your past, including failures, titles, recognitions, pretending: clean your heart so that He can come in and make everything new again.

Receive now the presence of the Lord inside of you. He makes you strong, changes your character, and transforms you into a new person in the name of Jesus Christ.

Placing Emotions in the Right Place

When making major life decisions, we must use our intelligent faith and not our emotions, because they are deceiving and can lead us to a path of destruction. When choosing a life partner, when pursuing our dreams, when facing prejudice, we should not base our life accomplishments on "quicksand" (emotions) but on the Word of God.

Emotions fulfill an important role in our lives if placed correctly. For example, Moses and Miriam sang and danced after they and all the people of Israel crossed the Red Sea (Exodus 15). Once they had overcome their enemies, slavery, and left their miserable life behind, they celebrated and glorified God with great joy. By doing so, they put emotions, music, and dance in the right place at the right time. It was a reflection of their true happiness and joy, a sincere outcome of the great miracle they experienced. They were happy, indeed!

But when they had to cross the Red Sea, they did not sing or dance. They took actions of faith and trusted the Word of God. If they had kept on singing or crying on the edge of the Red Sea, Pharaoh and the Egyptian army would have destroyed them completely.

Emotions are not an effective tool for overcoming problems; intelligent faith is. The Holy Spirit guides us to know when and where it is best to use our emotions. However, these feelings should not form the foundation of your life. If you want to live a happy and successful life and overcome all obstacles that come your way, build your life upon the Word of God, and nothing will be able to bring you down.

Food for THOUGHT

Emotions can be deceiving and unstable. They work against you when it comes to solving problems and making important choices.

Look at your life and identify where you have been using your emotions instead of intelligent faith. Ask yourself what the consequences, the fruits of those actions are. Make a clear decision to place emotions in the right place.

Your Identity and Behavior

What is your identity? It is the essence of who you are: your personality, your thoughts, your characteristics. Our identity involves the way we think, feel, behave, and even the people with whom we feel a connection. Some things are very inherent to us. Other aspects will be shaped as we continue to have more and more experiences. The question is: What will we allow to mold our identity? What kind of thoughts will take root in our minds? Our behavior and choices will be affected by them.

Did you ever catch yourself wishing you acted differently? Did you ever want to lead a different lifestyle, or have a different way of seeing things? It could be that deep down you are not satisfied with the way things are. This desire for change is a part of who you are; it is a sense of justice inside of you. People do not stay the same. Either they develop and become better versions of themselves, or they move backwards to self-destructive attitudes and behaviors.

The interesting thing about behavior is that it is a clear reflection of the thoughts we have inside of us. It also reflects how we have or have not been investing in ourselves.

God knows our deepest thoughts. We cannot pretend before God. We cannot put on a mask; nobody can fool Him because He knows who we are.

When you live by faith, you please God. He teaches and guides you when you do not know what to do. When you have the Holy Spirit, which is the Spirit of Justice, He shows you the way. He makes you feel uncomfortable when you are heading the wrong way. The only thing He does not do is take you by the hand and say, "Come on, leave this place!" He does not force you; He speaks to you. It is up to you and me to give heed to His guidance or not.

Regardless of the place you were born, your physical characteristics, the language you speak, or your ethnic, social, religious background, you are a human being created in the image of God. We have the abilities, intelligence, and conditions to choose to seek God and follow His Word and behave like Him. But, if we do not behave like the living God, then we invalidate the wisdom and qualities He gave us, and we look even more unlike Him.

A good example is King David, a young man that behaved with wisdom (1 Samuel 18:14). His behavior showed the thoughts he nurtured inside of him, and it showed how much he invested in himself. King David sought God and had pleasure in meditating in His Word. His behavior revealed his wisdom, making him earn the respect of those around him, including his enemies.

Another great example is Noah, who "was a just man, perfect in his generations. Noah walked with God" (Genesis 6:9). Noah absorbed God's thoughts and wisdom and applied them in his life. He was so strong in his identity and character, that even when everyone around him was losing control, he remained confident, growing better and happier each day. Noah was a righteous man; he was just, honest. He decided to do what was right, and that made him perfect in a time when people were evil and perverse.

This is no different today. We hear about children suffering abuse, people that grow up traumatized because an evil man or woman took their childhood away.

Though it was normal to do evil in Noah's time, or it seemed customary to do what was wrong, He stood out because he decided to do good. Now, how can you have justice from God, living in this generation and choosing to be unjust?

Analyze your life right now, see what kind of identity and behavior you are building for yourself: people steal, do you steal as well? People lie, do you lie as well? People are corrupt, are you corrupt as well? People deceive, do you deceive as well?

If the answer is yes, then how can you have a just life? How can you have justice in life? How can you be righteous in this way? It is impossible.

God does not expect perfection, but righteousness from all of us.

"But Noah found grace in the eyes of the Lord." (Genesis 6:8) Do you know why? Because he was a righteous man in that generation, and God chose him and guided him to build an ark. Noah and his family survived the flood, not because he had status, position, or special privileges, but because he was righteous.

Can God serve justice to somebody that is unfair, to somebody that is unjust, dishonest? A betrayer, a cheat? No, God cannot.

What identity do you want for yourself? Do you want to become a better and improved version of yourself? Do you want to behave with wisdom and understanding and see God's justice in your life? Then reevaluate what thoughts you have been taking in, what words you have been embracing as your own. The closer you get to God and His Word, the more you seek the Spirit of Faith, the more you will invest in who you are and the stronger you will be to stand for what is just, for what is right.

Body Language and What It Says About You

What is body language? It is the messages given through gestures, changes in facial expressions, it is when you show an angry face, a long face, when you make certain movements, all these together are your body language, which is communicating without words. In the same way that many spoken languages exist in the world, there is also the language of facial expressions, which is complemented by the way you speak and behave. All of these are conveying messages. They are representing you. They are expressing your emotions at that moment.

For example, if for any reason you make a mistake at work, and your boss calls you on it and you do not take it well, your facial expression changes, you become resentful, and you have this grumpy look on your face. This is the message you are passing on to others. Or it could be that your boss is testing you because they want to place you in a higher position with greater responsibilities. So, your employer decides to check your reactions and feedback and see how you will react to stressful situations. As a manager with greater responsibilities, you will have to be accountable and know how to deal with difficult issues.

When having your mistakes pointed out and corrected, which is something small, you change your facial expression, lose your temper, and speak angrily. Then your employer sees that you cannot handle being in a position with higher demands. They know that you will not manage it well because of your reactions.

What has your body language said about you? Has it closed the doors of opportunities before you because of your reactions? Has your body language expressed feelings of defeat, insecurity, and fears? Your body speaks without saying words, and this language communicates to others and could send messages you do not want. I encourage you to be attentive to your thoughts and body language. Work on changing your thoughts, speak words that empower you. Work also in shaping your body language to express your goals and aspirations.

YOU ARE A HUMAN BEING CREATED IN THE IMAGE OF GOD.

Other People's Perceptions

Recalling what was mentioned in Chapter 2, the best way to deal with prejudice is allowing people to know the truth, sharing who you are, letting them see their misconceptions. The best way to deal with discrimination is succeeding in life, achieving your goals.

I want to go back to our behavior, as a Black man that was once judged by the color of my skin. Perhaps you have been wrongfully judged solely by your skin tone. And maybe some people have also judged you by your behavior.

You have probably noticed that when a Black person does something wrong, people usually associate the mistake with the color of their skin. They say, "They do this because they are Black." Let's be honest: Is this true or false?

Specific adverse incidents happen, and some people usually say, "It had to be a Black person." Unfortunately, because of racism, everyone ends up being wrongfully judged due to the behavior of a few. When a Black person values themselves, some people even within the Black community say, "They are White on the inside." What they actually mean to say is that they know when to speak and when to listen and how to behave respectfully.

However, these respectful and righteous attitudes are not connected to the color of one's skin. It is not our skin color that defines us, but the choices we make in life. Regardless of external differences, our choices and behavior reveal who we are inside; they show the state of our soul, and remember, <u>the soul has no color</u>.

How can we change this situation? How can we change this story? There is only one way: by having good manners, respect, and consideration for others. Our behavior speaks for us. You can choose to be a reference, not a stereotype; you can choose to value and believe in yourself.

Therefore, value yourself, invest in your interior and it will reflect in your behavior. Change the way you answer people, your facial expressions. You are a person who thinks and who knows how to express yourself. Each one of us must know how to present ourselves and how to behave in a way that values who we are.

Be Yourself – Authenticity, Sincerity

Nowadays, many people will behave like someone else to flee discrimination and avoid being the victims of prejudice. They pretend to have different identities and personalities, and they try to change their skin tone, their hair color, their eye color, and even their facial features with the sole purpose of becoming someone they are not.

Here is the key to this message: do not pretend to be who you are not.

When you pretend to be someone you are not, you make matters worse. You make yourself look ridiculous. And the entire process is extremely tiring, living each day pretending and lying so that others will accept you. Being authentic is much better. You can stop pretending and begin believing and investing in yourself. This does not mean that you will not change for the better, but you will not change the wrong things for the wrong reasons.

Instead, you will make improvements within, in your character, to become a better version of you.

I want to say to you that you can overcome and succeed while being yourself. Your skin tone should not be a barrier. The color of your eyes, the shape of your nose, and the texture of your hair are not and will not be barriers to your success. Your background and education or your upbringing will not block you. The greatest obstacle, the biggest challenge, is inside of you—it is in your mind.

Do not allow outside pressure to keep you from being authentic, believing in yourself, and valuing who you are. Be yourself, and God will honor you. You can!

How to Invest in Yourself

Many people invest their money in banks. Many invest in the stock market, in real estate and assets to prepare for their future. However, the best investment that exists is to invest in oneself.

STOP
PRETENDING
AND BE
YOURSELF. BELIEVE
AND INVEST
IN YOU.

In the United States, if a person has a lot of money but does not have good credit, they will not be able to go very far. This person can have a lot of money, but if they do not have a good record, they will be limited and will not be able to accomplish many things.

How do people build their credit history? They purchase using credit cards and paying them off. The intention is not to develop debts but to establish a good credit history. When a person manages their accounts well and pays them on time, they earn points, reflecting their credibility. When a person does not pay their accounts on time, their credit score loses points. When they neglect to pay their bills, then these overdue accounts are sent to collection agencies, and that person will have bad credit for many years. They can even make a lot of money but will not be able to finance anything in the United States.

Now bringing this to our personal lives, many people have lacked this credibility in their own lives because they do not value themselves. They do not invest in themselves, in the way they speak, their future, or their behavior, and end up losing credibility with their family and themselves.

We must build good credit in all aspects, including our personal lives, with family and friends, education, financial goals, business, workplace, and in our community. Little by little, we will earn the respect of those around us.

Believe and invest in yourself. Invest in your spiritual life, in being free from any mental slavery. Use intelligent faith (see Chapter 3) to overcome obstacles and improve your character. Value your word and your presence, invest in being a person of your word, and in making a positive difference wherever you go. Invest in your mind, thoughts, and behavior by doing what is right, even when everyone around you is doing what is unjust. Invest in your future by pursuing your dreams and taking the necessary actions, and making the efforts needed to accomplish them. Do not draw back; move forward, you can! Finish the race, get yourself in that first-place spot on the podium. Regardless of any injustice against you, through an intelligent faith, you will succeed.

So, dear friends, you must invest in yourself. People will not be able to undervalue you because you will have presence, authority, and credibility.

I say to you once more: You can succeed and achieve regardless of the prejudice you have faced because of the color of your skin, origin, background, physical abilities, or any outward distinction. Invest in your potential, invest in your self-credit, and surely you will make a great difference wherever you go and in whatever you do.

Food for THOUGHT

What thoughts have you allowed to shape your identity and your behavior? What changes have you made intending to appear to be someone you are not in order to please other people? Have you been making the wrong changes for the wrong reasons? Ask yourself these questions. God believes in you. Now it is time for you to believe in yourself too.

Invest in your character, talents, and self-credit. You can do that with the guidance of the Spirit of Faith. If you take the first step, God will help you.

Next Generation

After God, your family comes next. Not your job, money, or career. After Jesus comes your family. Our family is our most important asset. When you invest in your family, you invest in your future. When you neglect your family, you are in reality neglecting yourself. When you despise your children, wife, or husband, you are despising yourself. Worse than prejudice, discrimination, racism, and injustice imposed on you, is having a broken family.

Invest in your spouse and your children. With an intelligent faith in the living God and a strong family, you do not need to "eat out of other people's hands" and depend on them. You can overcome and succeed regardless of any discrimination.

My wife Ima and I on our wedding day

Our children: Samela, and Samuel with his wife Hevilyn

My Family

My father was not raised in a home. He did not have a home. He came from a failed family. His father abandoned the family, and my dad had to start working at the age of 12. He became the man of the house, taking care of his mother and siblings.

When he was about to get married to my mother, his then brother-in-law made the following bet with him on his wedding day: "Let's see who will remain married for the longest: you or me. I come from a solid family. You, on the other hand, did not have a father. Your family is in shambles."

At that moment, he made a vow to himself, saying, "I did not have a father, but I will be the father I never had, and I will have the family I never had." And, so it happened. He always made efforts to be a good father and take care of his wife and children.

The examples my father gave us were the greatest life teachings my siblings and I had, and that we keep to this day.

One funny example that comes to mind is the time when, as a young boy, I decided to pick up a toy that was not mine from the street and take it home. My father saw it and knew that he had not bought it and that I did not have money to buy it either. He pulled my ear and walked me to the place where I picked up that toy. I left it there and never did something similar again. That structure and discipline my father taught me helped shape my character.

Today, I have a family. I have been married for 28 years. I made my vows to my wife, she made her vows to me, and we have a son and daughter. Our son recently married and began his own family.

After my salvation, the most valuable treasure I have is not my work, it is not my position as a spiritual leader, but it is my family. Without my family, I could not be the man of God I am today.

I invest in my family and I take care of them. In my home I am not a reverend, pastor, bishop, or missionary; I am a husband and father, and I invest in my family with all my strength.

I am not talking about what I do not have; I am giving you what I have. I am a man who is married to one woman. My children grew up to be wholesome, happy people. That required effort on my part, self-denial and sacrifice for the sake of my family. Those were investments that have paid off and today I am reaping the results. You too can do the same. If you have not done so until now, it is not too late. Start today, right now, because the person that has a family, has a stronghold. Without family, one does not have anything.

Investing in Your Family Is Investing in Your Heritage

You know, nowadays, people don't have families because they give more of themselves to their work, their studies, or their careers, than to their family.

Families today sit in the living room when they come together, but everybody is on their computers or cell phones, or with parents in the living room and the children in the bedroom, always preoccupied with technology. They do not have family conversations anymore because everybody is online. Now they have some online conference or text each other even when they sit together. They don't talk anymore.

Jesus talks about two houses. One built on sand and another on the rock (Matthew 7:24-27). Do not build your family on sand. Do not let your family be like today's modern family, which spends more time on their gadgets and personal interests than interacting with each other. You know that the old-fashioned family was much better; its value is more significant than what we see today.

Nowadays children kill their parents. Family values have been put down. They have been trashed.

Do not build your family on the sand. Sooner or later, this family will fall apart. Prison is full of people from broken homes, broken families, with absent fathers and mothers. Families built on sand, quicksand, that were swallowed by this world.

Do you have children? Take care of them. If you say good things about your children, if you bless them, they shall be blessed. If you are married, take care of your marriage. If you do not take care of your family, you are losing your life, you are losing yourself. God chose you to be the pillar of your family. Despite the circumstances you face and the past choices you made, you can decide today to invest in your marriage, in your children, and make a difference in the lives of your loved ones. You can!

If you want to have a stable family, follow the proven steps mentioned in the Bible. If you read Psalm 128, you are going to see order, discipline, and you are going to see your family based on the Word of God. If you read Ephesians, Galatians, you will see the principles of the family.

I don't mean a religious family; I am talking about the principles to have a solid and united family. To have love and respect between parents and children and between husband and wife. The husband and wife taking care of each other and their children as instructed by God's Word.

I always say: A family that prays together, stays together. However, before praying, set the example through your life. The best prayer is being a good example. If you pray and pray, but do not set a good example for your children, your prayer will be fruitless.

> *"Believe on the Lord Jesus Christ,*
> *and you will be saved, you and*
> *your household."*
> *(Acts 16:31)*

This statement requires an intelligent faith to put the Word of God into practice. By doing so, your family will be built upon the ROCK, and it will remain standing and strong under any storm of life coming your way.

WORSE THAN ANY DISCRIMINATION IS TO HAVE A BROKEN FAMILY.

Food for THOUGHT

If you have been placing career, personal projects, friends, addiction, or even a hobby, above your family, decide right now to STOP neglecting them and destroying your future with your own hands. You CAN be the husband, wife, father, and mother that will make a difference in your family. Build your household on the ROCK, on God's Word. Make Jesus the foundation of your home. Worse than any prejudice is to have a broken family. When you take care of your family, you are actually investing in your own future.

Writing a New Story

Perhaps up until now your story has been a story of pain and tears. You know well what injustice means because your heart carries the scars caused by it. I want you to know that you can change your story. Regardless of the color of your skin, origin, or background, whenever you want, you can overcome anything and be a happy and successful person.

All the great heroes of faith mentioned in the Bible endured humiliation and suffered discrimination during their journey. They were the last, yet through faith, they became the first. They wrote a new story for themselves.

The process of writing a new story is not an easy one. It requires a lot of effort, and it will seem like you are going against the current. You will face many obstacles. However, if you follow the steps provided here, I am confident that you will achieve a new story for yourself and your family.

> "Behold, I will do a new thing, (...) I will even make a road in the wilderness and rivers in the desert."
> (Isaiah 43:19)

This river represents your life. God wants to make your life spring forth with happiness, joy, and achievements, even amid the desert of injustices you have faced until now. You are not alone in this; take the first step, and He will help you along the way.

Leave the Past Behind and Look Ahead

People tend to say, "Back in the day," when talking about the old days. They even cry, feel sad, or depressed when they think of the past. Are you frequently digging up your past and bringing it to the present? This is a big mistake. Why? Because, when you bring the past to the present, you get stuck and you cannot move into the future.

You know, many people are bound to the past, making it impossible for them to move forward and improve their lives. God did not place our eyes on the back of our heads, but on the front for us to move ahead, not backward. Perhaps have been some episodes in your life that brought you disappointment and frustration, and whenever you remember those episodes, the things of the past, you move one step back in life. It is a problem for many people. You do not move forward in life because you dwell on your past relationships and past failures.

One day you might have pronounced a word wrong, or you did not know how to present yourself, and others then humiliated you, laughed at you. Now you have become shy, isolating yourself and nurturing many insecurities. You now have two options of either carrying this weight, this burden and reliving the scene in your mind, or you could leave it in the past, move ahead and say, "I failed and was humiliated, but I will prove to everyone that my God is alive and that I can succeed." Regrettably, many people choose the first option.

What God has for you is NOT in the PAST but in the FUTURE.

*"Do not remember the former things,
nor consider the things of old."*
(Isaiah 43:18)

Do yourself a favor: stop looking backwards. Stop looking at what happened yesterday, last week, last month.

Do not dwell on the past. Our lives have three phases: our past, present, and future. And no one can return to the past to change it.

We cannot move back in time. Life is always forward, but if you do not forget the things of the past, you are going to be stuck and afraid, fearful, and doubtful.

Place your past where it belongs: in the past and not the present. The past is over; move forward because what God has for you is in the future. What God has for you is in front of you, not behind you. Let it go. Only by doing so can you have a brighter future and a blessed present.

If you failed an exam, had a bad presentation or performance and felt humiliated, forget about it! Move on, move ahead and try again, this time around you will do much better. You will earn an excellent score because God is with you.

We are now living in the second phase: the present. Our present will determine how our future will be. For many of you, the future will be as terrible as the past was and the present has been. Why? Because you dwell on the past. You are moving back, reliving the old days, former sufferings, and old problems.

If you do not clean up your past, if you do not let go of your past, it is going to destroy you, it is going to mess up your future and the future of the new generation.

Perhaps you suffered in the past, and you continue to carry that pain and suffering in the present. This means that you did not overcome those problems and that they are going to be passed on to the next generation. Your children have a greater chance of having the same issues you had.

If you hold on to resentments and hatred, you are drinking your own poison because anger, hatred, and grudges are poisons that are killing you.

Do not drink your own poison. Throw it away! Forgive, let go of this situation, and surely you will become a happier and better person.

You should ask God to erase your past hurts from your memories. Only God has the power to clean up your past and bless your present so that your future may increase abundantly with happiness, prosperity, and accomplishments.

Work on Your Present

Many people say, "I already tried everything!" No, there is still something more that depends on you and that you must do. The apostle Paul said, "I have fought the good fight, I have finished the race, I have kept the faith" (2 Timothy 4:7).

Therefore, do not say that you did everything when you have not achieved what you wanted. You have not achieved it yet because you have not done everything. Continue working towards it.

Do not blame anybody. We are what we sow. You will sow today and reap tomorrow. If you sow the wrong seeds, you are going to reap the wrong fruits. It depends on you. If you sow goodness, that is what you will reap. If you sow forgiveness, you will ultimately reap forgiveness. If you sow obedience to the Word of God, which is the word of truth, love, justice, and faith, you will reap peace within and wisdom to achieve your goals regardless of any obstacles or circumstances.

You are going to sow new seeds, new choices, new decisions, so that in the future you may have a blessed life, a good life.

Good Lemonade

Faith gives us the ability to make lemonade out of lemons. When a person has the Spirit of Faith, although they have lemons (adverse events), which are sour, their faith makes sweet lemonade from these lemons. They suffer injustice but use that experience to make a difference in their lives and the lives of others. They face prejudice and obstacles, but they overcome them through their faith.

Instead of focusing on problems, they use their faith to look for and find the solution.

I do not know what your current situation is, but let's make a good lemonade out of this sour situation. If you failed once or twice, make sweet lemonade out of that lemon, make something good come out of it.

This is what faith does. Jacob was in a sour situation, but through his faith, his life became good lemonade. He was in distress, he had to run away from his father-in-law who was exploiting him, he was haunted by his own past mistakes and afraid of his brother's vengeance, but during all this turmoil he found deliverance and peace in God's presence. He literally wrestled with God for his blessing and prevailed (Genesis 32:22-28). You too can fight for a new story, a new identity in God's presence.

Put God First

Many people say, "I don't have time... I don't have time to read the Bible... I don't have time to pray, to seek God." But, if you notice, the time people spend on their cellphones, interacting on social networks, Facebook, WhatsApp, or Instagram... If they took this time and applied it to their spiritual life, they would be stronger people.

If you want to be a stronger person, invest in your spiritual life. Everybody faces problems. But the difference between the strong and the weak is that when you're strong, when you hear bad news, you take your case before God. You challenge Him and put all your efforts and strength into obeying Him and seeking His answer. You persevere, struggle, and insist on God, and He reverses the situation.

God can help you change your story entirely regardless of your background or origin. He raises people from the dust because He created the human being from the dust. This is what God does.

Maybe you have lost everything and everyone. Your life is in shambles, you lost everything, and you are now on the ground. Only Jesus has the power to raise you from the dust. God has the power to raise you from the ground and give you not a small life but abundant life.

The majority of people are busy and only think of God when facing trouble, but it's a priority to make time for Him regardless of whether you are facing big problems or not. So, place your relationship with God and your spiritual life before the accomplishments and things you want to conquer, before everything and everyone. All the other areas of your life depend on your spiritual life. It is your strong foundation that will help you stand amid any situation that comes your way.

Put Your Goals in Writing

Begin changing your life from the moment you start writing, literally, your new story. This is the homework that you will begin working on today. Get a notebook, a computer, whatever you wish, and begin writing your new story. I want you to define your vision and purpose, and set goals for yourself.

I want to guide you in understanding something very important: God's vision is higher than yours. Let me explain: When you are down in the valley, at a lower level, you only see what is around you. Your sight is limited. However, if you go to the highest place, to the peak of the mountain, from there you can have a better view. This is how God sees you. This is how God sees your future. He does not see you in the valley.

Again, when you are at a lower level, you only see what is there. But from above, you can see far into the horizon, and this is what God has for you.

Do not limit your goals, do not think small. Write down great and marvelous things because nothing is impossible for the God of the Bible, and He has great plans for you. Write down your vision and goals for every area of your life.

Make a Plan

Your success also depends on how much you plan. After all, we plan for what we believe in, for what we are sure will take place. If inside of you there is a certainty, a faith in that what you wrote down will take place, then now you will plan the steps to achieve it.

Take the time right now to think of each goal you wrote for each area of your life and ask God for His guidance. Write down the everyday actions you need to take to see your vision become a reality.

Remember, intelligent faith requires action. Wishful thinking and praying alone are not enough to see the results of your faith.

Move Ahead and Do Not Draw Back

Many people quit along the way. Many people begin things in life, but they never conclude them. When we look back, we see many people that have stopped along the way. People that started a career and made choices in life without seeing through the end.

Abraham, a hero of faith, did not give up. He began his journey and did not stop until it was complete. Abraham could not have children, but God made him the father of many nations (Romans 4:18). And this is what God wants. He wants you to reach the end. He does not want you to stop along the way.

Maybe what you want is taking a long time, longer than you expected.

> "Now the just shall live by faith; but if anyone draws back, My soul has no pleasure in him."
> (Hebrews 10:38)

Never draw back regardless of the obstacles you face. God has no pleasure in those who draw back. Move forward and God will be with you and help you along the way.

Do not pay attention to people's opinions. Do not bother yourself with what they say about you. If you worry about what people say, you are not going to move forward.

Believe in God, believe in yourself, and move ahead. Tackle each one of the steps in your plan to reach your goals and do not look back. You CAN and will succeed!

Have you been living in the past and regretting what has happened to you? Decide right now to let go and move forward. Say it, write it down, and be sure that your future will not be a reflection of your past. Remember this date, because today will mark a before and after in your life. Do not be afraid, your faith in practice will get you to the other side of this ocean of obstacles. You can and will make it.

It Is Just the Beginning

Let's go back to the question stated at the beginning of this book: what do you think of yourself now? How do you see yourself?

I pray and hope that by now you see yourself as God sees you: an overcomer, someone who has value beyond appearances. I pray and hope that the topics we mentioned have encouraged you to base your decisions and judgments on the content and not on the appearance of things, on an intelligent faith and not emotions.

I pray and hope, that as you journeyed with me through the pages of this book, you have realized that the soul has no color. That the essence of who we are is not our physical bodies. That you have understood that there is a bondage that holds people back from moving forward in life:

mental slavery and self-discrimination. That you have learned that faith has no color and that the Spirit of Faith has the power to take a person from dust, from the ash heap, to sit with princes (1 Samuel 2:8).

The Spirit of Faith does not differentiate between people based on appearances, but on their sincerity and the actions they take to seek God and trust and obey His Word. The Spirit of Faith is not an emotion or a good feeling, but a Power that God puts inside of you to guide you to victory in all aspects of life.

You have learned to invest in yourself and your family, to let go of the past, to change your thoughts, and to do today what will transform your future for the better.

I encourage you to take all the steps you learned here and apply them to your life. Let's make a challenge, yes a challenge!

Take each step attentively and put what you have learned into practice. However, you need to truly put effort into it. I am available to help you.

Feel free to reach out to me by sending an e-mail to bbf@universal.org. I will be glad to assist you with any questions and concerns.

May the God of the Bible bless all of you!

 Bira Fonseca, also known as Bishop Joshua, has dedicated over 30 years of his life to helping others as a minister, public speaker, and counselor. Alongside his wife Ima, he has worked with families in the United States, Brazil, and South Africa.

In his first book, Bira Fonseca draws from his experiences of facing racism throughout his life and his journey in finding his true value. He has also witnessed hundreds of life stories and situations of people from different walks of life.

On his UCAN events, Bira Fonseca has spoken in several US states and the Caribbean. One of these movements reached approximately ten thousand people: the "I Have a Dream" Concert at Madison Square Garden and in Brooklyn, NY, in celebration of Martin Luther King Jr. Day in 2016, with the participation of the African Choir from Soweto. On that occasion, he showed the importance of recognizing and breaking free from the mental slavery that imprisons many people today.

This has been one of his main goals: Helping people become free from within and create a new story for themselves. He achieves this through his daily TV show, aired on the Universal Living Faith Network, video and written blogs, social media, and ongoing communication with thousands of viewers.

He is an ordinary man who through faith in God and himself, has accomplished extraordinary results in his life, maintaining his core message to his viewers, "Yes, you CAN!"

# Stay Connected

Send me an e-mail at:
bbf@universal.org

Check out my blog:
birafonseca.com

Follow my show on Facebook:
Showdown of Faith

Watch the Showdown of Faith daily on the Universal Living Faith Network:
ulfn.org